4
INGREDIENTS

CHOCOLATE,

CAKES

&

CUTE THINGS

4 INGREDIENTS

Chocolate, CAKES & CUTE THINGS

SIMPLE, SWEET & SAVORY BITES
PERFECT *for* ENTERTAINING *at* HOME

Kim McCosker

ATRIA PAPERBACK

NEW YORK   LONDON   TORONTO   SYDNEY   NEW DELHI

Also by
KIM McCOSKER

4 INGREDIENTS KIDS
Simple, Healthy Fun in the Kitchen

4 INGREDIENTS ONE POT, ONE BOWL
Rediscover the Wonders of Simple, Home-Cooked Meals

4 INGREDIENTS CHRISTMAS
Recipes for a Simply Yummy Holiday

BABY BOWL
Home-Cooked Meals for Happy, Healthy Babies and Toddlers

By KIM McCOSKER & RACHAEL BERMINGHAM

4 INGREDIENTS
More Than 400 Quick, Easy, and Delicious Recipes Using 4 or Fewer Ingredients

4 INGREDIENTS GLUTEN-FREE
More Than 400 New and Exciting Gluten-Free Recipes Using 4 or Fewer Ingredients

ATRIA PAPERBACK

A Division of Simon & Schuster, Inc.

1230 Avenue of the Americas

New York, NY 10020

First Atria Paperback edition April 2014

ATRIA PAPERBACK and colophon are trademarks of Simon & Schuster, Inc.

For information about special discounts for bulk purchases, please contact Simon & Schuster Special Sales at 1-866-506-1949 or business@simonandschuster.com.

The Simon & Schuster Speakers Bureau can bring authors to your live event. For more information or to book an event, contact the Simon & Schuster Speakers Bureau at 1-866-248-3049 or visit our website at www.simonspeakers.com.

Photography by Megan Slade/info@meganslade.com

Interior design by Jane Archer/www.psbella.com

Manufactured in China

10 9 8 7 6 5 4 3 2 1

Library of Congress Cataloging-in-Publication Data

McCosker, Kim.
  4 ingredients chocolate, cakes & cute things : simple, sweet & savory bites perfect for entertaining at home / Kim McCosker.
     pages cm
Includes index.
1. Desserts. 2. Snack foods. 3. Quick and easy cooking.
I. Title. II. Title: Four ingredients chocolate, cakes and cute things.
  TX773.M16 2014
  641.86—dc23
                            2013029541

ISBN 978-1-4516-3568-3
ISBN 978-1-4516-3570-6 (ebook)

Contents

Contents

CUTE THINGS

INTRODUCTION

I don't know about you, but whenever I envision the menu for a wedding shower, a baby shower, or a simple yet luxurious afternoon tea with friends, my mind immediately goes to chocolate, cakes, and cute things. Divine Caramel Choc Truffles, beautifully whipped Fresh Raspberry Buttercream, and delightful Little Lemon Cheesecakes. Add to that some melt-in-your-mouth, savory-delicious Brie & Quince Tarts, Mini Salmon Quiches, and Pesto Palmiers, and, like magic, you have a glorious party spread that will put smiles on the faces of even your littlest guests.

If you are at all familiar with the 4 Ingredients series, you know that I am all about coming up with clever ways to simplify, diversify, and economize feeding your family healthfully and happily. *4 Ingredients Chocolate, Cakes & Cute Things* takes these ideas beyond the family table and out onto the veranda, your poolside patio, roof deck, living room, game room, even around the kitchen island. That place, wherever it may be, where your family and friends come together to celebrate and where you like to entertain.

Kid-proof an otherwise grown-up Sunday brunch by transforming a simple breakfast dish into Funny Face Bacon & Eggs. Refresh a summertime cocktail party with filled-to-the-rim glasses of Frosted Grapes in Bubbles. Treat a mom-to-be with a simple yet sinful Sponge Cake (which I craved throughout my pregnancy) and a fancy-looking (but couldn't be easier) Pretty Pavlova. Liven up a neighborhood block party with modern twists on classic favorites: Coney Island Meatballs, Pastrami "Tacos," and Peanut Butter & Jelly Cookies.

As in my previous books, the approximately 80 recipes in *4 Ingredients Chocolate, Cakes & Cute Things* all contain no more than 4 ingredients (salt, pepper, and water are not included). This means less money and energy spent on food, preparation, and cleanup and more time for you to enjoy the pleasures of hosting, whether it be for a gaggle of girlfriends, a business cocktail party, or a sweet birthday gathering for Grandma.

Spending time with the people you love is a gift. Consider *4 Ingredients Chocolate, Cakes & Cute Things* my gift to you! May you find comfort and inspiration, and make and share many delights from the pages within.

With love, Kim
xoxoxo

WORKING WITH CHOCOLATE

Know Your Chocolate

Never again do you have to look at an array of chocolates and ask yourself, "What's the difference?"

COCOA POWDER: Cacao beans are roasted, then cracked and winnowed, their outer shells blown away, to create cacao nibs. The cacao nibs are crushed and ground into a thick paste called "chocolate liquor" (there is no alcohol in it). Cocoa powder remains when cocoa butter (which is used to make solid chocolate) is removed from the paste. It is then ground and packaged as unsweetened cocoa powder, which is used in baking and other recipes. It can also be sweetened to make hot chocolate.

BITTERSWEET CHOCOLATE: Similar to unsweetened chocolate, just a little sweeter. I use them interchangeably. Unsweetened and bittersweet chocolate are used for recipes that call for other sweet ingredients like sugar, honey, or syrups to offset their bitter tastes.

SEMISWEET MORSELS (CHIPS): Everybody loves chocolate chip cookies. If you are making them, reach for the semisweet chocolate morsels or chips. They hold their shape and are not bitter. Once you bite into them, they melt into sweet goodness. Use them also for muffins and pancakes.

SEMISWEET CHOCOLATE BLOCKS: Primarily sold as baking chocolate. The chunks can be cut up and melted for candy, cakes, and icings.

MILK CHOCOLATE: Great for eating. Sugar, cocoa butter, vanilla, and milk are added to mask the bitterness of raw chocolate. Milk chocolate has more milk and sugar than dark chocolate or semisweet chocolate.

WHITE CHOCOLATE: Commonly consists of cocoa butter and sugar, but no cocoa.

Handling Chocolate

For best results, remember two words—LOW & SLOW!

ALWAYS MELT CHOCOLATE SLOWLY, at a low temperature. The melting point of chocolate is between 86° and 90°F, lower than body temperature.

NEVER LET THE TEMPERATURE OF YOUR CHOCOLATE GET ABOVE 115°F. Milk and white chocolates, which are more heat sensitive, should not be heated above 110°F.

MELTING CHOCOLATE—MICROWAVE: Chop into small pieces. In a clean, dry microwaveable dish, melt the chocolate on medium power in 30-second increments, stirring well after each, until melted.

MELTING CHOCOLATE—STOVETOP: Chop into small pieces and place in the top of a double boiler over hot, but not boiling, water. Stir until melted.

WATER AND CHOCOLATE: Chocolate is an oil-based product and oil and water don't mix. Melted chocolate responds noticeably to small amounts of moisture by transforming it from a shiny, smooth texture to a lumpy, grainy mass (called seizing).

TEMPERING CHOCOLATE: Tempering is necessary if you want to make professional-quality candies and truffles. When you melt chocolate, the molecules of fat separate. In order to put them back together, you must temper the chocolate. Tempering is a heating, cooling, and stirring process that induces the melted chocolate to set with a glossy surface and smooth texture. Chocolate is tempered when its temperature is between 84° and 88°F.

STORING CHOCOLATE: Store chocolate, well wrapped, in a cool dark place (65°F is ideal). If storage conditions are too cold, chocolate will "sweat" when brought to room temperature. If conditions are too warm, the cocoa butter will start to melt out, and a gray "bloom" will form on the surface. This doesn't affect the flavor of the chocolate, just its look.

Working with Cakes

MEASURE EVERYTHING. Recipes for baked goodies are usually an exact formula. Adding a pinch of this and a splash of that can lead to disaster.

FOR OPTIMUM HEIGHT AND TEXTURE, cake ingredients should be at room temperature prior to mixing. Eggs and butter from the refrigerator usually need about 1 hour to reach room temperature.

TO CREAM BUTTER AND SUGAR, make sure you combine thoroughly until the mixture is pale. Do the same when you beat eggs. This means you've beaten in lots of air, which is essential for a well-risen cake. Overmixing results in tough baked goods, so unless otherwise specified, after adding the flour, mix the dough only until blended.

USE A METAL SPOON rather than wooden (which retains moisture) to stir cake batters. Cut and fold the mixture with a metal spoon to keep the air in.

PREHEAT THE OVEN. Cakes should be placed straight into a hot oven to make sure they're tall and fluffy; it's that first blast of heat that makes the air bubbles in the batter expand quickly, causing the cake to rise.

DO NOT OPEN THE OVEN DOOR until the cake is more than halfway through its baking time. If you interrupt that initial rising stage, your cake could collapse.

TO COOL A CAKE, remove it from the oven and let it cool in the pan on a wire rack for 10 minutes.

IF YOU DON'T HAVE SELF-RISING FLOUR, for every 1 cup, combine 2 teaspoons baking powder, a pinch of salt, and 1 cup all-purpose flour.

CHOCOLATE

Caramel Choc Truffles

One of my boys' favorites. Make a double batch as they freeze well. You'll thank me later!

1 CAN (13.4 OUNCES) DULCE DE LECHE

2 TABLESPOONS BUTTER

1½ CUPS FINELY CRUSHED CHOCOLATE WAFER COOKIES

¾ CUP UNSWEETENED SHREDDED COCONUT

In a large saucepan, combine the dulce de leche and butter and bring to a gentle boil, stirring. Remove from the heat and let cool for 10 minutes. Add the crushed cookies and mix well. Refrigerate for 1 hour. Roll heaping teaspoons of the mixture into balls, roll in the coconut, and refrigerate until firm. Store in an airtight container in the fridge.

Choc Mint Leaves

Served chilled, these are a perfect way to end the evening with a lovely cup of tea or coffee.

3½ OUNCES SEMISWEET CHOCOLATE, COARSELY CHOPPED

16 FRESH MINT LEAVES, WASHED AND WELL DRIED

Line a baking sheet with wax paper. In a microwaveable bowl, melt the chocolate on medium power in 30-second increments, stirring after each, until smooth and creamy. One at a time, dip one side of each leaf into the chocolate, allowing the excess to drip back into the bowl. Place the leaves, chocolate side up, on the prepared sheet. Refrigerate until set. Gently peel the mint leaf from the chocolate and discard before serving. Store in an airtight container in the fridge.

Giant Freckles

Makes
8

I've yet to meet a child who doesn't like a giant freckle!

7 OUNCES MILK CHOCOLATE, COARSELY CHOPPED

½ CUP SPRINKLES

In a microwaveable bowl, melt the chocolate on medium power in 30-second increments, stirring after each, until smooth and creamy. Pour the chocolate into lollipop molds and insert sticks if using. Allow to set for a few minutes before covering with sprinkles. Alternatively, you could place lightly greased cookie cutters on a baking sheet lined with wax paper, spoon the melted chocolate into each, and top with the sprinkles. Refrigerate until set completely. Gently remove cookie cutters to serve.

Grape Clusters

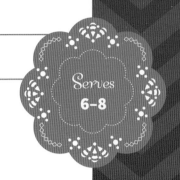

This recipe is great with or without the nuts. If you prefer, you can swap the hazelnuts for crushed pistachios, shredded coconut, or a little bit of peanut butter!

¼ POUND GREEN GRAPES, WASHED AND WELL DRIED

½ CUP ROASTED HAZELNUTS, COARSELY CHOPPED

3½ OUNCES BITTERSWEET CHOCOLATE, COARSELY CHOPPED

1 TABLESPOON NUTELLA

Cut the grape stems into clusters of 3 or 4 grapes. Line a baking sheet with wax paper and spread the chopped hazelnuts on a plate. In a microwaveable bowl, melt the chocolate and Nutella on medium power in 30-second increments, stirring after each, until smooth and creamy. Dip each grape cluster three-fourths of the way into the chocolate mixture, allowing the excess to drip back into the bowl. Then dip each cluster into the chopped nuts. Place on the prepared sheet. Pop into the fridge until set.

I'm "Nuts" for These!

Satisfy any craving with this versatile snack. A great movie-night-at-home treat.

3½ OUNCES SEMISWEET CHOCOLATE, COARSELY CHOPPED

1 CUP ROASTED ALMONDS

1 CUP PECAN HALVES

Line a baking sheet with wax paper. In a microwaveable bowl, melt the chocolate on medium power in 30-second increments, stirring after each, until smooth and creamy. Add the almonds to the melted chocolate and stir to completely coat each nut. Using a fork, remove them one at a time, and place on the baking sheet. Dip each pecan halfway into the remaining chocolate and place on the prepared sheet. Refrigerate until set.

Tip

Waste not if you want more! Pour leftover melted chocolate into molds and top with crushed nuts or sprinkles.

"La Dolce Vita" Pudding

This is comfort food at its finest!

4 CROISSANTS, QUARTERED

1 CUP RASPBERRY JAM

3½ OUNCES WHITE CHOCOLATE, COARSELY CHOPPED

7 OUNCES THICK STORE-BOUGHT CUSTARD

Preheat the oven to 350°F. Spread each croissant quarter with jam. Place the pieces, open side up, into a baking dish. Sprinkle with the chocolate then pour the custard over the top. Bake until the top is golden brown and the custard heated through, 12 to 15 minutes. This delicious treat can be made in one dish or in 4 individual ramekins (as in the photo). Top with fresh berries if desired.

Tip

Make your own custard easily by whisking 2 eggs and 3 tablespoons cornstarch into 3 cups of milk until smooth. Then over medium heat continue whisking until the custard thickens. Remove from heat and whisk in 3 to 4 tablespoons of sugar.

Mississippi Mud Drops

Balls of chocolate and Jell-O combine to form a delicious symphony in your mouth.

18- TO 20-OUNCE STORE-BOUGHT MOIST FUDGE CAKE WITH CHOCOLATE FROSTING

7 OUNCES MILK CHOCOLATE, COARSELY CHOPPED

2 PACKAGES (3 OUNCES EACH) RASPBERRY GELATIN DESSERT

Line 2 baking sheets with wax paper. Crumble the cake and icing into a large bowl and mix well until combined. Using a teaspoon, roll the mixture firmly into balls. Chill in the freezer for 20 minutes. In a microwaveable bowl, melt the chocolate on medium power in 30-second increments, stirring after each, until smooth and creamy. Spread the gelatin crystals out on a flat plate. Dip one ball at a time into the melted chocolate, allowing the excess to drip back into the bowl, then place onto the prepared sheets. Pop into the freezer for 20 minutes to set. Remove and let stand for 2 to 3 minutes to sweat slightly. Then roll into the gelatin to decorate. Store in an airtight container in the fridge.

Mounds Bar Balls

This heavenly combination of creamy chocolate and moist coconut always transports me to some tropical island, where I'm tall and thin, wearing a grass skirt and a lei, swaying rhythmically to the beat. . . . Then I wake up!

4 CUPS UNSWEETENED SHREDDED COCONUT, PLUS MORE FOR GARNISH

1 CAN (14 OUNCES) CONDENSED MILK

7 OUNCES BITTERSWEET CHOCOLATE, COARSELY CHOPPED

1 TABLESPOON VEGETABLE OIL

In a large bowl, mix together the coconut and condensed milk. Using a teaspoon, roll the mixture into balls and place on 2 baking sheets. Place the balls in the freezer to chill until hard. In a microwaveable bowl, melt the chocolate on medium power in 30-second increments, stirring after each, until smooth and creamy. Add the oil and stir until combined. Remove the balls from the freezer and dip, one at a time, into the melted chocolate. Return to the baking sheets and decorate with a sprinkle of unsweetened shredded coconut. Refrigerate until set. Store in an airtight container in the fridge.

Oreo Candies

These are a wonderful party gift. Decorate with chocolate transfer sheets (as in the photo) or shredded coconut, sprinkles, edible glitter, or a drizzle of bittersweet chocolate.

9 OUNCES WHITE CHOCOLATE, COARSELY CHOPPED

12 OREO COOKIES

12 CHOCOLATE TRANSFER SHEETS

Line a baking sheet with wax paper. In a microwaveable bowl, melt the chocolate on medium power in 30-second increments, stirring after each, until smooth and creamy. Brush excess crumbs off the cookies, then with a fork dip each Oreo cookie into the melted chocolate, turning to completely cover. Allow the excess chocolate to drip back into the bowl, then place on the baking sheet. When all the cookies are covered, lay a transfer sheet carefully on top of each, covering its upper surface. Let the chocolate set at room temperature and then peel off the transfer sheet.

Fun Fact

18 million pounds of cocoa and 47 million pounds of cream filling are used each year to make Oreos!

Peanut Butter Balls

I dare you to try stopping at just one; it's almost impossible! I often make these when I want to say "thank you" to someone special in my family's life—a kind neighbor, a patient teacher, or someone who deserves something special to cheer up her day.

14 OUNCES SEMISWEET CHOCOLATE, COARSELY CHOPPED

¼ CUP CRUNCHY PEANUT BUTTER

1 CUP COARSELY CHOPPED PEANUTS

In a saucepan, combine 7 ounces of the chocolate and the peanut butter. Stir constantly over low heat until melted and combined. Pour the mixture into a small bowl and refrigerate for 1 hour to firm up. Line a baking sheet with wax paper. Roll teaspoons of the chilled chocolate mixture into balls and place on the baking sheet. Place in the freezer for 1 hour. In a microwaveable bowl, melt the remaining 7 ounces chocolate on medium power in 30-second increments, stirring after each, until smooth and creamy. Place the peanuts into a small bowl near the melted chocolate. Remove the balls from the freezer and dip, one at a time, in the melted chocolate, then roll in the peanuts. Place back on the cold baking sheet and refrigerate until set. Store in an airtight container in the fridge.

Peppermint Slice

A beautiful combination of chocolate and mint. Perfect for holiday gatherings or as party favors, teacher gifts, or an afternoon treat.

Makes
24 squares

7 OUNCES BITTERSWEET CHOCOLATE CHIPS

3 DROPS PEPPERMINT EXTRACT

3½ OUNCES WHITE CHOCOLATE CHIPS

4 DROPS GREEN FOOD COLORING

Line an 8-inch square cake pan with wax paper. In a double boiler, melt the dark chocolate chips over simmering, not boiling, water. Stir until smooth. Add the peppermint extract and stir to combine. Spread half the mixture evenly over the bottom of the prepared pan. Set in the fridge for 5 minutes. Melt the white chocolate chips the same way, then stir in the food coloring. Spread this over the layer of dark chocolate and refrigerate until set, 30 minutes. Spread the remaining dark chocolate over the green-white chocolate and return to the fridge to set, 40 minutes. Remove from the pan and using a long, thin knife dipped first in boiling water and then dried, cut into squares and store in an airtight container in the fridge.

Polka Dot Circus Balls

I make this recipe regularly to use up leftover chocolate. It's just a bonus that everyone happens to love them.

9 OUNCES SEMISWEET CHOCOLATE, COARSELY CHOPPED

¼ CUP HEAVY CREAM

1 CUP SPRINKLES

In a microwaveable bowl, melt the chocolate with the cream on medium power in 30-second increments, stirring after each, until the mixture (called a ganache) is smooth and creamy. Place in the fridge to cool and firm up. When the ganache is almost set, scoop a teaspoon of the mixture and gently roll into a ball, then roll in the sprinkles to coat. Continue until all the mixture is gone. Store in an airtight container in the fridge.

Optional
Mix raisins, dried blueberries, or nuts into the ganache before refrigerating.

Rocky Road Truffles

Makes 24

Rocky Road was invented in Australia in 1853 and is our gift to the world. Rocky Road Truffles were invented by my beautiful friend Melanie Roberts and are her gift to us!

14 OUNCES WHITE CHOCOLATE, COARSELY CHOPPED

¼ CUP HEAVY CREAM

2 OUNCES TURKISH DELIGHT (OR MARSHMALLOWS OR BOTH), FINELY CHOPPED

½ CUP CHOPPED PISTACHIOS, PLUS MORE FOR GARNISH

Optional
Drizzle with a little pink candy coating. (I bought it in a tube . . . shhhh!)

Line a baking sheet with wax paper. In a microwaveable bowl, melt 7 ounces of the chocolate with the cream on medium power in 30-second increments, stirring after each, until the mixture is smooth and creamy. Allow to cool slightly before adding the Turkish delight and pistachios, then mix well. Refrigerate for 1 hour, or until firm. Remove from the fridge and roll teaspoons of the mixture into balls, then place on the baking sheet. Freeze for 1 hour. Melt the remaining 7 ounces chocolate in the microwave on medium power in 30-second intervals, stirring after each, until melted and smooth. Remove the balls from the freezer. Using a fork, dip one at a time into the white chocolate. Allow excess chocolate to drip back into the bowl. Place back on the baking sheet and sprinkle with a few slivers of pistachio. Repeat until all truffles are coated. Refrigerate until set. Store in an airtight container in the fridge.

Snakes Alive

This is super easy and fun to make with your children. Serve at their next birthday party and watch the squirms and giggles begin!

3½ OUNCES MILK CHOCOLATE, COARSELY CHOPPED

12 GUMMI SNAKES (MAYBE MORE DEPENDING ON SIZE)

Line a baking sheet with wax paper. In a microwaveable bowl, melt the chocolate on medium power in 30-second increments, stirring after each, until smooth and creamy. Dip three-fourths of each snake into the chocolate, letting the excess drip back into the bowl. Place on the baking sheet and refrigerate until set.

Optional
If you can't find snakes, rainbow Twizzlers work just as nicely.

White Chocolate Pretzels

These are an easy treat for holiday gatherings. Turn little pretzel sticks into spiders for a Halloween party or snowflakes for New Year's!

4 OUNCES WHITE CHOCOLATE, COARSELY CHOPPED

1 TABLESPOON CRUNCHY PEANUT BUTTER

4 OUNCES PRETZELS (STICKS OR TRADITIONAL SHAPES)

Line a baking sheet with wax paper. In a microwaveable bowl, melt the chocolate with the peanut butter on medium power in 30-second increments, stirring after each, until the mixture is smooth and creamy. Dip each pretzel in the chocolate, coating some, half coating others, then place on the baking sheet. When all have been dipped, place in the refrigerator to set.

CAKES

1,1,1,1 Cake

This is quite simply one of my all-time favorite cakes because of its versatility. If you don't like coconut, swap in ½ cup cocoa for an easy chocolate cake; or just keep both the cocoa and coconut for a Choc-Coconut Cake.

1 CUP UNSWEETENED SHREDDED COCONUT

1 CUP WHOLE MILK

1 CUP SUPERFINE SUGAR

1 CUP SELF-RISING FLOUR

Position a rack in the lower third of the oven and preheat to 350°F. Line a 9 x 5-inch loaf pan with parchment paper. In a large bowl, stir together all the ingredients until well combined. Pour the batter into the pan and bake until a wooden skewer inserted into the center comes out clean, 40 to 45 minutes.

Optional

Top this with delicious Citrus Cream Cheese Frosting: Combine 1 cup confectioners' sugar, 3 ounces cream cheese, 3 tablespoons butter, 1 teaspoon orange juice, and 1 tablespoon grated orange zest. That's it, deliciously simple!

Apple Cookie Cake

A cool, fresh, delightful alternative to a more traditional cobbler or crumble.

1½ STICKS (6 OUNCES) BUTTER, MELTED

1 BOX (16 OUNCES) WHITE CAKE MIX

1½ CUPS (14 OUNCES) CANNED APPLE PIE FILLING

1 CUP SOUR CREAM

Preheat the oven to 350°F. Line the bottom of a 10-inch round cake pan with parchment paper. In a bowl, stir together the melted butter and cake mix to form a stiff dough. Spread evenly in the pan and bake for 15 minutes. Meanwhile, in a small bowl, stir together the apple pie filling and sour cream. Take the cake out of the oven and spread the apple mixture evenly on top. Return the cake to the oven for another 15 minutes. Let cool at room temperature for 15 minutes, then cool completely in the refrigerator. Slice and serve cold. Garnish with finely sliced apples if desired.

Optional

Sprinkle with cinnamon before the final bake or choose an apple pie filling with cinnamon. Ever since I learned that cinnamon is good for our brains, I'm adding it to everything!

Tip

Stewed apples are really just as easy to prepare as buying canned apple pie filling at the store. Peel and slice 4 apples and place them into a saucepan. Cover with water, sprinkle with sugar, and bring to a boil. Reduce the heat, cover, and simmer until tender, 8 to 10 minutes. Drain any excess liquid and cool.

Buttercream Frosting

The rich, satiny texture of this basic buttercream is your launch pad into heaven!

3 CUPS CONFECTIONERS' SUGAR

1½ STICKS (6 OUNCES) BUTTER, AT ROOM TEMPERATURE

1 TEASPOON VANILLA EXTRACT

2 TABLESPOONS HEAVY CREAM

In a bowl, with an electric mixer on low speed, beat together the sugar and butter until well blended, then increase the speed to medium and beat for another 3 minutes. Add vanilla and cream and beat on medium speed for 1 minute more, adding more cream if needed to achieve a spreadable consistency.

Optional

Add cocoa powder (a little for light, a lot for dark) to make a Chocolate Buttercream. Or, for a Strawberry Buttercream, add 1 cup freeze-dried strawberries, pulverized to a powder in a food processor. To make a Creamy PB Buttercream, combine ¾ cup creamy peanut butter, ¼ cup heavy cream, 2 tablespoons butter, and mix well. Add 1 cup confectioners' sugar, more if needed.

Butterscotch Pumpkin Pie

A perfect way to transition from summer into autumn.
A delicious ending to a Sunday dinner or a yummy, slightly
more sophisticated Halloween party centerpiece.

2 LARGE EGGS

**1 PINT TOFFEE OR DULCE DE LECHE
ICE CREAM, SOFTENED**

**1¼ CUPS CANNED UNSWEETENED
PUMPKIN PUREE**

1 REFRIGERATED 9-INCH PIE CRUST

Preheat the oven to 350°F. In a bowl, with an
electric mixer, beat the eggs until pale and
frothy. Add the ice cream and pumpkin. Stir
until well combined and smooth. Pour into
the pie crust and bake until the filling is set,
about 40 minutes. Cool and enjoy!

Cheaters' Cheesecake

Serves 16

It's not cheating if they don't know (shhhhhhhhhhh)! This is such a quick and easy option when you just don't have time but still need a real WOW treat!

1 STORE-BOUGHT CHEESECAKE (I LOVE COSTCO'S 5-POUND MONSTER . . . SOOOO GOOOOD!)

TOPPING OF CHOICE (SEE RECIPE)

Slice the cheesecake and serve with one of the following toppings. (If you aren't serving a big crowd, slice only half the cheesecake and freeze the remainder.)

Zingy Grape Topping: Halve grapes and drizzle with lime juice.

Chocolate Cherry Delight: Chocolate-covered cherries.

Hot Butterscotch Pecan Sauce: In a saucepan, melt 4 tablespoons (½ stick) butter and 6 tablespoons brown sugar. Stir in ½ cup chopped pecans and cook over medium heat to a sticky yummy syrup.

Summer Berry Treat: Pile each slice high with fresh, seasonal berries, whole and sliced, and a dollop of whipped cream on the side.

Tip

To make nice, clean slices, do so while the cake is still partially frozen. Dip a large, sharp knife into very hot water, dry quickly and slice.

Chocolate Mousse Cupcakes

Makes
6

In previous centuries, before muffin tins were widely available, little cakes were often baked in individual pottery cups, ramekins, or molds and took their name from the "cups" they were baked in. "Cupcake" is the name now given to any small cake that is about the size of a teacup.

1½ CUPS MILK CHOCOLATE CHIPS

3 LARGE EGGS

¼ CUP SELF-RISING FLOUR

1½ CUPS WHIPPED CREAM, FOR SERVING

Preheat the oven to 350°F. In a small saucepan, melt the chocolate over low heat, stirring often until smooth. Remove from the heat. In a small bowl, whisk together the eggs and flour. Stir the egg mixture into the chocolate. Line 6 cups of a muffin tin with paper liners. Divide the batter among the cups and bake until the top and sides are set but the center is still liquid, about 20 minutes. Allow to cool in the pan for 10 minutes. Top with a dollop of whipped cream to serve.

Optional
Sprinkle shaved chocolate on the cream to make these look even more dazzling!

Coconut & Mango Crepe Cake

Coconut is such a great flavor. Add mango to the mix and you have a midsummer night's dream! I also used fresh lime to complement the other flavors.

4 MANGOES

1 CAN (14 OUNCES) COCONUT CREAM, WHIPPED

6 CREPES (9-INCH STORE-BOUGHT)

1 LIME

Peel and slice the mangoes. Set aside 2 tablespoons coconut cream and a couple slices of mango for decoration. Lay one crepe on a serving plate. Top with a layer of whipped coconut cream, then mango, and finally a sprinkling of grated lime zest. Top with another crepe and continue layering until all ingredients are used. Set in the fridge for 1 hour. Decorate the top with the reserved cream and mango. Garnish with slices of lime and cut into wedges to serve.

Tip

Make your own absolutely delectable Mangoes en Miel (Mango Syrup):
Simply peel 4 small mangoes, leaving them whole.
Place in a small saucepan and cover with water. Add ½ cup brown sugar
and bring to a boil, stirring to dissolve the sugar. Add 1 cinnamon stick
and reduce the heat. Cover and simmer for 1 hour. Cool, remove the seeds, then
layer: crepes, mangoes en miel, coconut cream, and lime zest.

Cookies & Cream Ice Cream Cake

This recipe is so easy to make and is unbelievably delicious.
If you are a fan of Oreo cookies, you simply must try it.

2½ CUPS HEAVY CREAM, CHILLED

1 CAN (14 OUNCES) CONDENSED MILK, CHILLED

14 OREO COOKIES, ROUGHLY BROKEN

Line a 9 x 5-inch loaf pan with wax paper. In a large bowl, with an electric mixer, beat the cream until stiff peaks start to form. Add the condensed milk and beat on low speed for 1 minute, or until well combined. Fold in three-fourths of the broken cookies, the remainder will be used for garnish when ready to serve. Pour the mixture into the loaf pan, cover with plastic wrap, and freeze overnight. Remove from the freezer 10 minutes before serving. To serve, invert onto a rectangular serving plate, gently peel the wax paper away, and decorate with the remaining cookies.

Creamy Nutella Frosting

The word "delicious" does not do this frosting justice. Increase or decrease the amount of Nutella based on your sweet tooth.

2 STICKS (8 OUNCES) UNSALTED BUTTER, AT ROOM TEMPERATURE

2 CUPS CONFECTIONERS' SUGAR

¾ CUP NUTELLA

3 TABLESPOONS HEAVY CREAM

In a bowl, with an electric mixer, beat the butter on medium speed for 2 to 3 minutes, until smooth and creamy. You want a very creamy base before adding anything else. Add the sugar and continue to beat on medium speed. The mixture will be fairly thick. Add the Nutella and beat on medium speed. Add the cream and beat to combine. If the frosting is too thick, add more heavy cream (1 tablespoon at a time). If the frosting is too thin, add more sugar (¼ cup at a time). Taste the frosting and add salt to cut the sweetness (I added about ¼ teaspoon).

Date & Walnut Muffins

This delectable treat is full of fiber, flavor, and protein. Can I have two, please?

2 TEASPOONS INSTANT COFFEE GRANULES

13 OUNCES PITTED DATES, CHOPPED

1 CUP SELF-RISING FLOUR

¾ CUP CHOPPED WALNUTS

In a small bowl, stir together the coffee and 1 cup boiling water. Add the dates to the bowl and let soak for at least 2 hours. Preheat the oven to 350°F. Line 12 cups of a muffin tin with paper liners. Stir the flour and walnuts into the date mixture. Divide the batter among the muffin cups and bake until a wooden skewer inserted into the center of a muffin comes out clean, about 30 minutes.

Tip

To beautify these moist muffins, my gorgeous friend Leonie made "button flowers" with her 5-year-old daughter, Ruby. They cut flowers from pretty cardboard and glued a button in the center. They then stuck them to the pink crepe paper that we wrapped around the muffins. Minimal effort for maximum impact!

Deliciously Devonshire Sandwich Cake

This recipe is pure bliss during a summertime tea. For extra wow, add a tablespoon of Bailey's to the cream.

1 PULLMAN OR SANDWICH LOAF, UNSLICED

1 CUP STRAWBERRY JAM

2½ CUPS HEAVY CREAM, WHIPPED

Tip

Rose petals, in all varieties, are not only beautiful but edible. Darker colors provide more pronounced flavors. As seen in the photo, cut a blueberry into quarters (without cutting all the way through), place it gently into just the right spot, and dot it with a pinch of fresh raspberry and a mint leaf so that it looks like a beautiful little flower. Too cute!

Line the bottom and the 2 long sides of a 9 x 5-inch loaf pan with wax paper with overhang for easy removal. Trim the crust off each side of the loaf and discard. Cut the remaining bread into 3 long rectangular 1-inch-thick slices to fit within the pan. Place a slice in the bottom of the pan and top with one-third of the jam and one-third of the whipped cream. Repeat the layering 2 more times. Using a flat blade knife, smooth the top layer of cream. Cover with plastic wrap and freeze for 4 hours. Remove and transfer to a serving platter. Slice while still frozen, then thaw before serving.

Lemon Cupcakes

You know you are onto a good thing when after just one bite you are asked, "How did you make this?" The awkward bit is trying to make the recipe sound more difficult than it actually is! Cassandra van Breugel, I can't thank you enough for sharing this recipe with me.

1 CUP SELF-RISING FLOUR

⅔ CUP LEMON CURD

1 CAN (14 OUNCES) CONDENSED MILK

1 LARGE EGG

Preheat the oven to 350°F. Sift the flour into a bowl and add the remaining ingredients. Beat with an electric mixer for 2 minutes until pale and fluffy. Line 12 cups of a muffin tin with decorative paper liners and divide the batter among the cups. Bake until a wooden skewer inserted in the center of a cupcake comes out clean, 15 minutes.

Optional
Top with Raspberry Buttercream (page 72).

Little Lemon Cheesecakes

Makes
12

These addictive cheesecakes are often made by teenager Liam Evans when he needs to bribe his parents (which is often). I hear it works every time!

12 CRUNCHY, BUTTERY ROUND COOKIES (THE SAME DIAMETER AS THE BOTTOM OF A MUFFIN CUP)

9 OUNCES CREAM CHEESE, AT ROOM TEMPERATURE

1 JAR (10 OUNCES) LEMON CURD

1 CUP BLUEBERRIES

Line 12 cups of a muffin tin with paper liners and place one cookie, flat side up, into each. Using an electric mixer, beat the cream cheese until creamy. Add all the lemon curd and continue mixing until smooth. Spoon the mixture onto the cookies and freeze for 2 to 3 hours, or until firm. Five minutes before serving, remove the liners and decorate with fresh blueberries.

Marshmallow Fondant

Thank you to Stefanie Bamford for sharing this recipe on my 4 Ingredients Facebook page. I was in the office and read it out to the girls. It silenced us. All we could say was, "Wow!" And that was before we made it!

Makes enough for a 2-layer cake or 24 cupcakes

4 CUPS REGULAR MARSHMALLOWS

FOOD COLORING

8 CUPS (2 POUNDS 3 OUNCES) CONFECTIONERS' SUGAR, SIFTED

In a microwaveable bowl, combine the marshmallows and 2 tablespoons water and microwave for 1 to 2 minutes to melt the marshmallows. Stir to ensure all the marshmallows have melted. Add the food coloring. Slowly mix in 7 cups of the sifted confectioners' sugar; the "dough" will be very sticky and get very hard to mix. Lightly cover a work surface with a little extra confectioners' sugar, turn out the dough, and knead, working in the remaining 1 cup sugar until it forms a nonsticky dough. Wrap in plastic wrap and refrigerate for at least 3 hours or overnight. Bring to room temperature and re-knead to soften (you can microwave in 10-second increments to help). Roll out and use as desired.

Marshmallow Frosting

This is just lovely.

Makes enough to frost two **8**-inch layer cakes or **24** cupcakes

1 CUP OF GRANULATED SUGAR

½ TEASPOON CREAM OF TARTAR

4 EGG WHITES, AT ROOM TEMPERATURE

1 TEASPOON VANILLA EXTRACT

In a medium saucepan, add the sugar and cream of tartar to one-third cup of water. Do not stir the mixture as it will cause the sugar to crystallize. Boil just until thick clear bubbles appear (should only take about 4 to 5 minutes and reads a temperature of 245°F). Do not overboil. Meanwhile, in a bowl beat the egg whites until the mixture starts to thicken and forms soft peaks. Now, slowly add the hot syrup a little at a time and beat to combine, 7 minutes. In the last minute, add the vanilla. Use immediately.

Tip
You will get more volume when beating egg whites if you first bring them to room temperature.

Peanut Butter Ice Cream Pie

Who doesn't love peanut butter and ice cream? Combining the two is pure magic.

9 OUNCES CHOCOLATE WAFER COOKIES (OR CHOCOLATE GRAHAM CRACKERS)

1 STICK (4 OUNCES) BUTTER, MELTED

1 QUART VANILLA ICE CREAM, SOFTENED

1¼ CUPS CRUNCHY PEANUT BUTTER

Line an 8-inch pie plate with wax paper. Break the cookies into pieces and process in a food processor until finely crushed. Add the butter and mix well until thoroughly combined. Use the back of a metal spoon to press the cookie mixture evenly over the bottom of the pie plate. In a large bowl, with an electric mixer, beat together the ice cream and peanut butter until nice and smooth. Pour into the pie plate and place in the freezer for at least 4 hours. Remove from the freezer 10 minutes prior to serving.

Optional

Add 1 teaspoon cinnamon to the cookie base. Serve drizzled with a delectable Hot Fudge Sauce: In a microwaveable bowl, combine 7 ounces broken bittersweet chocolate, 1 cup large or small marshmallows, and 1 cup heavy cream. Microwave on medium power in 30-second increments, stirring after each, until smooth.

Pecan "Pie"

This is not at all like an actual pecan pie, but it is a quick and easy dessert with a lot of the same flavors—and it will delight and surprise your family and friends.

3 LARGE EGG WHITES, AT ROOM TEMPERATURE

1 CUP SUPERFINE SUGAR

1 CUP CHOPPED PECANS

22 RITZ CRACKERS, CRUSHED

Preheat the oven to 350°F. Line an 8-inch pie plate with parchment paper. In a bowl, with an electric mixer, beat the egg whites until soft peaks form, about 6 minutes. Add the sugar, 1 tablespoon at a time, beating well until the sugar is dissolved and the meringue is thick and glossy. Fold in the pecans and crushed crackers. Using a spatula, scrape the mixture into the prepared pie plate and bake until dry to the touch, about 25 minutes.

Optional
Serve with a dollop of whipped cream and sliced fresh strawberries.

Pretty Pavlova

Pavlova is one of Australia's and New Zealand's most popular desserts. Traditionally served topped with freshly whipped cream and seasonal fruits and berries. . . . Light and lovely!

6 LARGE EGG WHITES, AT ROOM TEMPERATURE

1½ CUPS SUPERFINE SUGAR

1 TABLESPOON CORNSTARCH

2 TEASPOONS DISTILLED WHITE VINEGAR

Optional

For the photo I added 1 teaspoon of pink food coloring to the last spoonful of sugar. To serve, I decorated with freshly whipped cream, sliced green grapes, and pretty rose petals.

Preheat the oven to 250°F. Trace an 8-inch circle onto parchment paper and place on a baking sheet. In a bowl, with an electric mixer, beat the egg whites until soft peaks form, about 10 minutes. Gradually beat in the sugar, 1 tablespoon at a time, beating well until the sugar is dissolved and the meringue is thick and glossy. Add the cornstarch and vinegar and whisk until combined. Pile the meringue onto the traced circle, shaping it into a large round disc. Bake until dry to the touch, about 1½ hours. Turn off the oven, crack the door open, and leave to cool completely.

Raspberry & Almond Cake

A versatile gluten-free cake that can be changed to suit any taste. Simply swap out the raspberries for stewed and pureed apples, bananas, or oranges. It's up to you!

2 CUPS FROZEN RASPBERRIES, THAWED

6 LARGE EGGS, AT ROOM TEMPERATURE

1 CUP SUPERFINE SUGAR

2¼ CUPS ALMOND MEAL

Preheat the oven to 320°F. Line the bottom of a 9-inch round cake pan with parchment paper. Puree the raspberries, seeds included, and set aside. In a bowl, with an electric mixer, beat the eggs and sugar until thick and glossy, about 10 minutes. Add the puree and almond meal and stir to combine. Pour into the cake pan and bake for 1 hour to 1 hour 10 minutes.

Note: This cake will sink after being removed from the oven since there is no flour to maintain the rise.

Optional

When ready to serve, fill the middle of the cake (where it sank) with a delicious frosting or freshly whipped cream and a sea of beautiful fresh berries. Divine!

Raspberry Buttercream

Makes enough to frost a large round cake or **24** cupcakes

Fresh or frozen raspberries can be used for this mouth-watering buttercream. I always have frozen raspberries in the freezer. They are economical, full of antioxidants, and sensational in morning smoothies.

12 OUNCES RASPBERRIES, FRESH OR FROZEN

1 STICK (4 OUNCES) UNSALTED BUTTER, AT ROOM TEMPERATURE

3½ CUPS CONFECTIONERS' SUGAR

½ TEASPOON FRESH LEMON JUICE

Optional

Another way to make a delish Raspberry Buttercream is to mix together 3 tablespoons softened butter, 2 cups confectioners' sugar, and 1 generous tablespoon raspberry jam. Simple!

In a small saucepan, heat the raspberries over medium heat, stirring frequently until they are broken down into a sauce. Pass the sauce through a fine-mesh sieve to remove the seeds, then pour the raspberry sauce back into the saucepan. Simmer until the sauce reduces to about ¼ cup. It will be a very rich and concentrated sauce. Set aside to cool. In a bowl, with an electric mixer, cream the butter on medium-high speed for 2 minutes, until lightened in color and fluffy. Add 2 cups of the sugar, the cooled raspberry sauce, and lemon juice. Continue mixing until smooth. Add the remaining 1½ cups sugar and mix until smooth.

Rocky Road Cake

Serves
8

I have made this cake for many special occasions. A little lace and ribbon and voilà! It's gorgeous! You can find Turkish Delight (which is a common confection in Australia and part of our Rocky Road) online.

10½ OUNCES MILK CHOCOLATE WITH ALMONDS, COARSELY CHOPPED

3½ OUNCES TURKISH DELIGHT, ROUGHLY CHOPPED

½ CUP REGULAR MARSHMALLOWS, HALVED

6 GRAHAM CRACKERS, BROKEN INTO PIECES

Line the bottoms of two 4-inch cake pans with wax paper. In a microwaveable bowl, melt the chocolate on medium power in 30-second increments, stirring after each, until smooth and creamy. Allow to cool for 5 minutes, then stir in the remaining ingredients, mixing well to combine. Divide the mixture evenly between the two pans and refrigerate until set. Slice to serve.

Optional

Rather than two smaller cakes, make one bigger using an 8-inch cake pan. Substitute red jellies or jujubes if you can't find Turkish Delight.

Sponge Cake

This is a longtime family favorite. When I was pregnant with my first baby, Morgan, I craved this cake. I can't tell you how many I made during that nine-month period. Maybe that's why he turned out so sweet?

4 LARGE EGGS, AT ROOM TEMPERATURE

¾ CUP SUPERFINE SUGAR

⅓ CUP CORNSTARCH, SIFTED 4 TIMES

⅔ CUP SELF-RISING FLOUR, SIFTED 4 TIMES

Optional

Serve with your favorite frosting or with freshly whipped cream, jam, and strawberries.

Position a rack in the bottom third of the oven and preheat to 375°F. Line two 8-inch cake pans with parchment paper. In a bowl, with an electric mixer, beat the eggs and sugar until thick, glossy, and tripled in volume, 10 minutes. Gradually sift cornstarch and flour mixture over egg mixture while simultaneously folding in with a large metal spoon until just combined. Divide mixture between prepared pans. Bake for 20 minutes, or until cakes have shrunk away from the sides slightly and spring back when gently touched. Place on wire racks, carefully peel away baking paper, then leave to cool.

CUTE THINGS

Savory

Bolognese Boats

This is such a cute way to transform a family favorite dinner—pasta with meat sauce—into a pretty appetizer when entertaining.

24 JUMBO PASTA SHELLS

2 CUPS BOTTLED MEATY PASTA SAUCE, SUCH AS BOLOGNESE

1 CUP FINELY GRATED PARMESAN CHEESE

In a large pot of salted boiling water, cook the pasta shells according to package directions. Drain and place on a baking sheet; allow to cool. Preheat the oven to 320°F. Fill each shell with 1 tablespoon pasta sauce and sprinkle with Parmesan. Bake until the sauce is warmed through and the cheese is golden, about 10 minutes.

Fun Fact

The earliest recorded use of "The Queen of Sauces" called "alla Bolognese," (pronounced: bo-lone-YAYZ-ay) comes from the fifth century. The name simply means "In the style of Bologna," as in the city.

Breakfast Cups

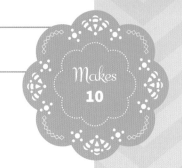

Customize these however you like: smoked salmon with cream cheese and fresh dill, Brie and cranberry sauce, ham and cheese. The options are endless, but I suggest trying two of my favorite fillings, as seen below.

10 SLICES WHOLE WHEAT SANDWICH BREAD

2 TABLESPOONS BUTTER, AT ROOM TEMPERATURE

CAFÉ-STYLE SCRAMBLED EGGS OR MORNING MUSHIES (RECIPES FOLLOW)

Preheat the oven to 350°F. Cut the crusts off the bread slices. (Freeze the crusts to use for breadcrumbs at a later date.) Roll over the bread gently with a rolling pin to flatten, then cut a round from each with a 3-inch cookie cutter. Butter each bread round on both sides and press each into the cup of a muffin tin. Bake until golden, 6 to 8 minutes.

Café-Style Scrambled Eggs

4 LARGE EGGS
½ CUP HEAVY CREAM

In a microwaveable dish, beat together the eggs and cream; season with salt and pepper to taste. Cook for 2½ minutes or until the eggs start to rise.

Morning Mushies

1 TEASPOON BUTTER
1 CUP SLICED BUTTON MUSHROOMS
½ CUP HEAVY CREAM

In a nonstick skillet, heat the butter over medium heat. Add the mushrooms and cook, stirring, for 3 minutes. Add the cream and gently stir until the sauce thickens, 4 minutes. Season to taste with sea salt and cracked black pepper.

Brie & Quince Tarts

Elegantly easy—music to my ears!

1 SHEET FROZEN PUFF PASTRY, THAWED BUT CHILLED

2.5 OUNCES BRIE CHEESE, CUT INTO 16 PIECES

3 OUNCES QUINCE PASTE, CHOPPED

Preheat the oven to 400°F. Roll the pastry out and use a 2-inch round cookie cutter to cut 16 rounds from the dough. Divide the rounds between 2 nonstick muffin tins and prick all over with a fork. Distribute the Brie pieces and quince paste evenly among the pastry rounds and season lightly with sea salt and pepper (to taste). Bake about 10 to 12 minutes or until crisp and golden. Remove the tarts from the oven and set aside to cool.

Cheese Triangles

Perennially popular.

3 LARGE EGGS

10 OUNCES FETA CHEESE

9 SHEETS FROZEN PHYLLO DOUGH, THAWED

1 STICK (4 OUNCES) BUTTER, MELTED

Preheat the oven to 400°F. Line a baking sheet with parchment paper. In a medium bowl, lightly beat the eggs. Crumble the feta into the bowl. Season with salt and pepper to taste and mix well. Remove 3 sheets of phyllo (covering the rest with a damp cloth to prevent them from drying out). Brush the first sheet of phyllo with melted butter. Top with a second sheet and brush with butter; repeat with the third sheet. Cut the pastry lengthwise into 4 strips, then crosswise in half so each strip is about 7 inches long. Place 2 teaspoons of the cheese mixture onto the bottom edge of each strip. Beginning at the bottom, cheese-coated edge, fold into a triangle and keep folding (like folding a flag), maintaining the triangular shape. Place on the baking sheet. Repeat the process, using the remaining phyllo and cheese mixture. Bake 10 to 12 minutes or until crisp and golden.

Coney Island Meatballs

Makes
20

Meatballs are not only popular but budget friendly; ground beef is one of the cheapest meats sold around the world. This recipe is easy and full of fabulous flavor.

1 POUND LEAN GROUND BEEF

½ CUP KETCHUP

½ CUP SHERRY

2 TABLESPOONS BROWN SUGAR

Preheat the oven to 375°F. Season the beef with salt and pepper to taste. Using a tablespoon, shape into meatballs. Place the meatballs into a nonstick frying pan and cook over medium heat, turning until brown all over. In a small bowl, stir together the ketchup, sherry, and brown sugar. Pour the sauce over the meatballs and bake for an additional 10 minutes. Serve the meatballs drizzled with the super delicious sauce.

Optional

I like to serve these sprinkled with lightly toasted sesame seeds and cilantro.

Curried Butternut Soup Bowls

This is a novel way to eat soup. Spoon it out, then enjoy the yummy bread bowl.

2 POUNDS BUTTERNUT SQUASH, PEELED AND CHOPPED

1 TEASPOON CURRY POWDER

12 SMALL ROUND HARD ROLLS, TOASTED

½ CUP HEAVY CREAM

Preheat the oven to 350°F. In a saucepan, combine the squash, 2 cups water, the curry, and sea salt and pepper to taste. Bring to a boil, then reduce to a simmer, and cook until tender, 20 to 25 minutes. Cut a lid from each roll and scoop out the filling. Place on a baking sheet and bake for 6 minutes to lightly toast. When the squash is tender, allow to cool a little. Then transfer it to a blender and puree until smooth. Stir in the cream. Spoon the soup into the toasted rolls to serve.

Optional

Finely chopped onion and a clove of minced garlic, sautéed together in olive oil, would also be a delicious addition to this dish. Fold it into the soup when you add the cream. My mouth is watering just thinking about it!

Dreamy Creamy Brie

Use whatever jam, jelly, or preserve you and your family enjoy.

4 SLICES WHOLE WHEAT BREAD

4-OUNCE WHEEL DOUBLE-CREAM BRIE CHEESE

2 TABLESPOONS RASPBERRY JAM

¼ CUP SLIVERED ALMONDS, TOASTED

Preheat the oven to 350°F. Remove the crusts from the bread slices (freeze the crusts for making breadcrumbs at a later date). Cut each piece of bread diagonally into quarters. Place on a baking sheet and bake until lightly golden and crisp, about 6 minutes. Meanwhile, place the Brie on a microwaveable serving plate, spread with the jam, and sprinkle the almonds over the top. Cook on high for 30 seconds, wait 5 seconds, repeat this process twice to prevent overheating the cheese on the inside. Serve with the toast points.

Funny Face Bacon & Eggs

A perfect dish for the kiddies during an otherwise grown-up brunch.

2 SLICES AMERICAN BACON

2 LARGE EGGS

2 SLICES BAGUETTE

In a small nonstick skillet, cook the bacon over medium heat until the fat starts to release into the pan and the bacon starts to turn crispy. Place 2 egg rings in the pan and break an egg into each. Cook to your liking and finish off under the broiler if you prefer the yolks cooked. Arrange the bacon (mouth and 1 slice for the eyebrows) and eggs (eyes) on the plate in the shape of a "Funny Face" that even "Babs" would be proud of. Serve with two slices of toasted baguette for the ears.

Lamb Samosas

Little parcels of deliciousness.

1 POUND LEAN GROUND LAMB

⅔ CUP BOTTLED TIKKA MASALA SIMMER SAUCE

12 SHEETS FROZEN PHYLLO DOUGH, THAWED

1 STICK (4 OUNCES) BUTTER, MELTED

Optional

I sprinkled these with poppy seeds before baking and served scattered with parsley and a sweet mango relish.

In a nonstick skillet, brown the ground lamb. Add the tikka masala sauce. Stir, reduce the heat and simmer for a few minutes, then set aside to cool. Preheat the oven to 380°F. Line a baking sheet with parchment paper. Remove 3 sheets of phyllo (covering the rest with a damp cloth to prevent them from drying out). Brush the first sheet of phyllo with melted butter. Top with a second sheet and brush with butter; repeat with the third sheet. Cut the pastry lengthwise into 4 strips, then in half so each strip is about 7 inches long. Place 2 teaspoons of the lamb mixture onto the bottom edge of each strip. Beginning at the bottom, filling-coated edge, fold into a triangle and keep folding (like folding a flag), maintaining the triangular shape. Place on the baking sheet. Make more samosas with the remaining phyllo and filling. Finally, baste with butter and bake until golden and crisp, about 20 minutes. Serve immediately.

Mini Salmon Quiches

Makes 24

Simple and stylish!

2 SHEETS FROZEN PUFF PASTRY, THAWED BUT CHILLED

8 OUNCES SMOKED SALMON PÂTÉ

½ CUP WHOLE MILK

3 LARGE EGGS

Preheat the oven to 400°F. With a 3-inch cookie cutter, cut 24 rounds out of the puff pastry. Use half the rounds to line 12 cups of a nonstick muffin tin. In a bowl or blender, beat together the pâté, milk, and eggs and season with cracked pepper. Divide the filling among the muffin cups. Bake until the filling is puffed and the pastry golden, about 30 minutes. Let stand for 10 minutes before removing from the pan. Repeat to make the second dozen.

Optional

Serve topped with a sprig of fresh dill or the grated zest of a lemon. Instead of pâté, try smoked salmon cream cheese.

Olive Tapenade

This is a super easy homemade tapenade. When you can buy kalamatas in bulk (and for a good price), make extra and bottle in a cute jar. Take a bit of remnant cloth, kitchen twine, or string, and label with a lovable gift tag.

⅔ CUP PITTED KALAMATA OLIVES

1 CLOVE GARLIC, SMASHED

2 TABLESPOONS CAPERS

1 TABLESPOON LEMON-INFUSED OR REGULAR OLIVE OIL

Place all the ingredients in a blender and process until relatively smooth. Store in an airtight jar in the refrigerator until needed.

Fun Fact

Olive trees are harvested every 15 years. Sound like a long time? It's nothing compared to the average age of an olive tree, 300 to 600 years.

Pastrami "Tacos"

A light, elegant alternative to a traditional deli meat sandwich spread. Try a colorful beet dip instead of hummus. These are incredibly versatile and just scrummy with any number of fresh, seasonal vegetables.

12 ROUND SLICES PASTRAMI

¼ CUP HUMMUS

1 AVOCADO, SLICED

1 SMALL HANDFUL SPROUTS OR WATERCRESS

Place each slice of pastrami on a flat surface. Spread with hummus and top with avocado and sprouts. Bring up opposite sides and stud with a toothpick to serve.

Optional

To make homemade Beet Dip, simply blend a 15-ounce can of baby beets, 8 ounces light cream cheese, 2 tablespoons lemon juice, 1 teaspoon each of ground cumin and coriander, and a pinch of sea salt and pepper.

Pesto Palmiers

I cannot count how many times people have asked me how I make these mouth-watering morsels.

1 SHEET FROZEN PUFF PASTRY, THAWED BUT CHILLED

½ CUP BASIL PESTO (SEE TIP)

¼ CUP GRATED PARMESAN CHEESE

Preheat the oven to 400°F. Line a baking sheet with parchment paper. Spread the pastry with pesto and then sprinkle with Parmesan. Season with cracked black pepper. Tightly roll up one long side until you reach the middle, then repeat with the other side. Carefully slice across the log into ½-inch slices. Arrange the palmiers on the baking sheet and pinch the bottom of each to form a heart shape. Bake until golden brown, 15 to 20 minutes.

Tip:

To make your own Basil Pesto: Simply combine ¼ cup toasted pine nuts, 1½ cups basil leaves, 2 garlic cloves, and ¾ cup shredded Parmesan in a blender. Blend while gradually adding 5 tablespoons olive oil.

Picnic Loaf

This is a recipe from my beautiful next-door neighbor, Michelle Dodd. Think of this simple idea when you next head out on your 4th of July picnic. Just fill it with the things your family loves to eat!

1 CIABATTA LOAF

14 OUNCES GIARDINIERA (ITALIAN PICKLED VEGETABLES), CHOPPED AND WELL DRAINED

8 BOCCONCINI BALLS, SLICED

3 OUNCES SLICED HAM, PEPPERONI, OR SALAMI

Split the ciabatta loaf lengthwise and scoop out the bread. Fill one side with the giardiniera. Fill the other side with bocconcini. Follow with your choice of ham, pepperoni, or salami. Place the halves back together, wrap tightly in parchment paper, and secure with masking tape or kitchen twine. Pop in the fridge with a weight on top (a casserole dish would do) and leave for 2 hours. To serve, simply unwrap and cut crosswise into slices.

Roasted Red Pepper Tartlets

Serve these during your next family movie or game night instead of ordering pizza. Add a kick of flavor by using a hot salsa.

1 SHEET FROZEN PUFF PASTRY, THAWED BUT CHILLED

1 CONTAINER (10 OUNCES) ROASTED PEPPER DIP OR SALSA

5 SLICES BOTTLED MARINATED ROASTED RED PEPPERS, CUT INTO THIN STRIPS

Preheat the oven to 400°F. Line a baking sheet with parchment paper. Cut the sheet of pastry into ten 3-inch squares. Lightly score a ½-inch border around the entire edge of each with a paring knife and then prick the pastry inside with a fork (the edges of each square will puff up while the centers will stay down). Divide the dip equally among the pastry centers, top with the peppers, and bake until puffed and golden, 15 to 20 minutes. Remove, cool slightly, and serve.

Optional

Scatter with fresh basil leaves if you have.

Salmon Bites

Makes
12

The perfect hors d'oeuvre for a Sunday brunch or bridal shower. They'll be gone in seconds!

2 LARGE PITA BREADS, SPLIT OPEN

½ CUP BASIL PESTO (PAGE 106)

6 BOCCONCINI BALLS, HALVED

2 OUNCES SMOKED SALMON, CUT INTO 12 STRIPS

Preheat the oven to 400°F. Using a 2-inch cookie cutter, cut 12 rounds from the pita breads. Spread each pita round evenly with pesto. Place a bocconcini half over the pesto. Place the bites on a baking sheet and bake until the pita is crisp and the cheese is melted, about 10 minutes. Remove from the oven and top each with a ribbon of smoked salmon and season with cracked pepper.

Optional

Scatter each with fresh dill to serve. Dill comes from the old English word dilla, meaning "to lull" because as a tea it was used to soothe stomach pains and colic in babies.

Sausage Rolls

These will be a hit at any gathering with men in attendance. Be they 6 or 76, boys love sausages—with or without fairy decorations!

2 SHEETS FROZEN PUFF PASTRY, THAWED BUT CHILLED

8 LINK SAUSAGES, COOKED AND CUT IN HALF

⅔ CUP KETCHUP

2 TABLESPOONS WORCESTERSHIRE SAUCE

Preheat the oven to 400°F. Cut the pastry sheets into squares the same dimension as the length of a sausage piece. Place a sausage piece at one end of the square. Brush the opposing edge with water and roll to enclose. Place on a baking sheet and bake until golden brown, about 20 minutes. Mix the sauces together and serve with the hot, flaky sausage rolls. Yummy!

Stuffed Button Mushrooms

Makes
16

Stuffed mushrooms make a delicious snack for any gathering. You can stuff them with meat, cheese, an herbed breadcrumb mixture, crab or shrimp. My personal fave is Boursin cheese mixed with chopped artichokes and roasted red peppers. Enjoy!

16 BUTTON MUSHROOMS

4 OUNCES BRIE CHEESE

½ CUP THAI SWEET CHILI SAUCE

Preheat the broiler. Brush and stem the mushrooms. Place a sliver of Brie over the mushroom and a dollop of chili sauce over the Brie. Arrange the mushrooms on a baking pan and broil until the cheese melts, 2 to 3 minutes.

Too Easy Syrup

This is fabulous drizzled over just about any grilled or poached fish or seafood dish.

2 CUPS SUPERFINE SUGAR

2 LEMONS

2 LIMES

RED PEPPER FLAKES

In a saucepan, combine 2 cups water, the sugar, and the whole lemons and limes. Bring to a boil, then reduce the heat and simmer for 30 minutes, allowing time for the flavors to blend. Remove from the heat, discard the whole lemons and limes. Stir in pepper flakes to taste and let cool for 30 minutes. Store in an airtight jar.

Veggie Kebabs

Kebabs are quick and easy for entertaining. Add whatever fruits or vegetables you have available, and make eating vegetables fun!

1 RED BELL PEPPER, CUT INTO CHUNKS

1 RED ONION, CUT INTO CHUNKS

¼ FRESH PINEAPPLE, CUT INTO CHUNKS

16 BUTTON MUSHROOMS, WASHED

If using wooden skewers, soak them in water for 30 minutes before grilling. Preheat the grill. Thread 8 skewers alternately with the ingredients. Grill until softened and heated through, 2 to 3 minutes on each side.

Optional
Serve drizzled with a yummy
Thai sweet chili sauce.

Apple Tarte Tatin

A classic recipe made simple. Two words: TRY IT.

4 TABLESPOONS (½ STICK) SALTED BUTTER

4 MEDIUM GREEN APPLES, PEELED, CORED, AND QUARTERED

½ CUP PACKED LIGHT BROWN SUGAR

1 SHEET FROZEN PUFF PASTRY, THAWED BUT CHILLED

Variation

Cut 12 rounds from the pastry and place into the cups of a buttered muffin tin. Place 2 or 3 apple quarters into each and drizzle with the sugar syrup. Bake for 10 to 12 minutes and serve with cream or ice cream.

Preheat the oven to 400°F. Line the bottom of an 8-inch round cake pan with parchment paper. In a large nonstick skillet, melt the butter. Add the apple quarters and cook, turning, until golden, about 4 minutes. Add the brown sugar and 2 tablespoons cold water. Cook and stir until the sugar has dissolved and a delicious syrup has formed, 2 to 3 minutes. Bring to a boil, then reduce the heat to low and simmer for 2 to 3 minutes to thicken the syrup. Arrange the apples in the cake pan. Drizzle that yummy syrup over the fruit. Cut a 9-inch round from the sheet of puff pastry and place over the apples, tucking in at the edges. Bake until the pastry is golden and puffed, about 15 minutes. Let sit for 5 minutes. Turn out onto a plate and slice to serve.

Amaretti Cookies

Makes
24

These little bites of loveliness are delightful served with a cup of tea or coffee.

2 CUPS ALMOND MEAL

1 TEASPOON ALMOND EXTRACT

¾ CUP SUPERFINE SUGAR

4 LARGE EGG WHITES

Preheat the oven to 375°F. Line a baking sheet with parchment paper. In a bowl, combine the almond meal, almond extract, and 9 tablespoons of the sugar. In a separate bowl, with an electric mixer, beat the egg whites until stiff peaks form, about 5 minutes. Gradually beat in the remaining 3 tablespoons sugar. Sprinkle one-third of the almond meal mixture over the egg whites and fold it in. Repeat with another one-third, and then the final third. Spoon the mixture into a piping bag fitted with a large plain tip (or sturdy resealable plastic bag with a ¼ -inch hole cut from one corner) and pipe walnut-sized dollops onto the baking sheet. Bake until golden, 15 minutes.

Bailey's Dip

Bailey's is just so versatile, you will love it as a dip with fresh seasonal fruit, but it is also resplendent in cheesecakes, ice creams, pies, and muffins. Oh! And have you seen the recipe on page 148?

¼ CUP BAILEY'S IRISH CREAM LIQUEUR

2 TABLESPOONS BROWN SUGAR

8 OUNCES SOUR CREAM

1 POUND STRAWBERRIES

In a bowl, mix together the Bailey's, brown sugar, and sour cream. Spoon into a serving dish and serve with fresh strawberries for dipping.

Tip:

To make your own Homemade Bailey's, take 2 cans (12 ounces each) evaporated milk, 1 can (14 ounces) condensed milk, 1 cup whiskey, and 3 tablespoons Hershey's chocolate syrup and blend together. Shake before using and serve over crushed ice.

Blueberry Cheesecake Ice Cream

Frozen blueberries work wonders in this amazing and amazingly versatile dessert, but so will any other fruit you have stored in the freezer. Try raspberries, blackberries, strawberries, or a mix of all three!

4 OUNCES SHORTBREAD COOKIES, BROKEN UP

3 CUPS FROZEN BLUEBERRIES

¼ CUP CONDENSED MILK

5 OUNCES CREAM CHEESE, AT ROOM TEMPERATURE

In a food processor or blender, process the cookies for 4 seconds. Add the blueberries, milk, and cream cheese and blend until nice and smooth. Serve immediately in a tall glass.

Optional

I garnished this yummy ice cream with a sliced blueberry and a little lavender—all that beautiful purple—too pretty!

Caramel Chews

Individually wrapping each caramel in cellophane, tied
with a ribbon and sealed with wax, make beautiful gifts.

**1 STICK (¼ POUND) BUTTER, PLUS
MORE FOR GREASING THE BAKING
DISH**

**¼ CUP PACKED LIGHT BROWN
SUGAR**

2 TABLESPOONS DARK CORN SYRUP

**¾ CUP PLUS 2 TABLESPOONS
(½ CAN) CONDENSED MILK**

Line an 8-inch square baking pan with wax
paper. In a saucepan, combine the stick of
butter, the brown sugar, corn syrup, and
condensed milk. Bring to a gentle boil and
boil for 15 minutes, stirring frequently to
prevent burning. Pour the mixture into the
prepared baking pan and refrigerate for at
least 2 hours. Cut into 16 squares, 4 across
and 4 down, and store in the fridge in an
airtight container.

Caramel Volcanic Apples

Makes
2

Baked apples are an age-old dessert that continues to stand the test of time because they are just delicious.

2 GRANNY SMITH APPLES

2 MILKY WAY BARS (1.84 OUNCES EACH), FROZEN AND HALVED LENGTHWISE

2 TABLESPOONS MUSCAT WINE

1 TEASPOON LIGHT BROWN SUGAR

Preheat the oven to 350°F. Core the apples almost through the bottom, but stopping short so the filling won't come out. Push a length of Milky Way bar into the middle. Place the apples in a baking pan and drizzle 1 tablespoon wine over each. Sprinkle with the brown sugar and bake for 20 minutes or until tender. Be prepared. . . this is like an exploding volcano of molten chocolate!

Optional
Serve with a generous scoop
of ice cream.

Chocsicles

Two ingredients that are fantastic on their own but when combined create MAGIC!

1½ CUPS CHOCOLATE MILK

½ CUP NUTELLA

6 WOODEN POPSICLE STICKS

In a bowl, with an electric mixer, beat together the chocolate milk and Nutella. Divide the mixture among 6 popsicle molds and put the sticks in place. Keep in the freezer until set.

Fun Fact

Nutella is a chocolate-hazelnut spread that was created in Italy in the 1940s by Pietro Ferrero. At that time, chocolate was in short supply because of the war, so he stretched what he had by adding ground hazelnuts. *Grazie,* Pietro, my boys thank you from the bottom of their gorgeously grubby little toes!

Cute Cookies

What I truly love about this recipe is you can add just about anything you like to it: sprinkles, chocolate chips, raisins, diced apple, corn flakes, M&M's (as I did in the photo), or keep it simple with a teaspoon of cinnamon.

1 CUP SUGAR

4 STICKS (1 POUND) BUTTER, AT ROOM TEMPERATURE

5 CUPS SELF-RISING FLOUR

1 CAN (14 OUNCES) CONDENSED MILK

In a bowl, with an electric mixer, cream the sugar and butter until pale and fluffy. Sift in the flour and pour in the condensed milk. Mix together, roll into a log, wrap in plastic wrap, and place in the freezer for 1 hour to firm up the dough for slicing. Preheat the oven to 350°F. Line 2 baking sheets with parchment paper. Remove the dough from the freezer and slice into ½-inch-thick discs, stud each with a chocolate chip or M&M (or several of each), and place 1 to 2 inches apart on the baking sheet. Bake until golden, 10 to 12 minutes.

Tip

If you don't want to make all the cookies in one go, divide the dough in half and roll into 2 logs. Bake up half and keep the other half in the freezer for up to a month. Thaw slightly before slicing.

Eton Mess

A traditional British dessert using just three ingredients. Eton Mess is usually made with strawberries, but you could also use raspberries, bananas, or pineapple.

½ POUND STRAWBERRIES, SLICED

4 OUNCES MERINGUES (STORE-BOUGHT OR HOMEMADE), BROKEN INTO CHUNKS

1 CUP HEAVY CREAM, WHIPPED

Gently mash some of the strawberries, leaving some sliced. Mix the strawberries together, then fold in the meringues and whipped cream. Spoon into serving glasses and serve with the sliced strawberries.

Optional
Add a dash of port or a splash of ginger cordial.

Frosted Grapes in Bubbles

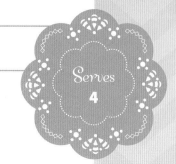

Serves
4

How super clever is this? The perfect summertime Champagne with bites of fruit. An added benefit—the frozen grapes keep my bubbles cooler longer!

8 SEEDLESS GRAPES, FROZEN

27 OUNCES CHAMPAGNE OR PROSECCO

Take 4 champagne flutes and drop 2 frozen grapes into each. Before pouring, tilt the glasses at a steep angle, then gently pour the Champagne down the side.

Ginger & Raisin Scones

Makes
12

This recipe reminds me of simpler days and the wonderful aromas of my beautiful grandmother's kitchen. Bake these and create your own special moments.

4 CUPS SELF-RISING FLOUR, PLUS MORE FOR THE WORK SURFACE

1¼ CUPS HEAVY CREAM

1 CUP GINGER ALE

½ CUP RAISINS

Optional
Serve with some freshly whipped cream, raspberry jam, or a simple blueberry jam.

Preheat the oven to 400°F. Line a baking sheet with parchment paper. Sift the flour into a large bowl. Create a well in the flour and add the cream, ginger ale, and raisins. Using a dinner knife, stir, cutting through the mixture to make a soft, pliable dough. Tip the dough out onto a floured surface and pat into a shape about 1-inch thick. Cut out the dough with a 2-inch round biscuit cutter, gather the scraps, pat out, and cut more. Arrange the rounds close together on the baking sheet. Bake until risen and golden in color, 12 to 13 minutes. These can be frozen for up to a month or simply halve the ingredients for a smaller batch.

Hit the Road Bars

These are great for lunch boxes, morning coffee, afternoon tea, or for those moments when you just need a little pick-me-up.

4 CUPS QUICK-COOKING OATS

2 CUPS RAW (SKIN-ON) ALMONDS, COARSELY CHOPPED

¾ CUP + 3 TABLESPOONS CONDENSED MILK

1 STICK (¼ POUND) BUTTER, MELTED

Preheat the oven to 320°F. Line a 9 x 13-inch baking pan with parchment paper. In a large bowl, combine all the oats, almonds, condensed milk, and melted butter. Spoon the mixture into the prepared pan and bake until golden, about 25 minutes. Let sit until slightly cooled, then cut into 24 bars while still warm. When cool, store in an airtight container.

Homemade Raspberry Jam

This recipe yields incredible results with minimal fuss. It is my one and only raspberry jam recipe. I hope your family likes it as much as mine does!

1 POUND (4 CUPS) FRESH RASPBERRIES

2 CUPS SUGAR

1 TEASPOON GRATED LEMON ZEST (OPTIONAL)

1 TABLESPOON FRESH LEMON JUICE (OPTIONAL)

In a large saucepan, heat the berries, crushing all the while, until they reach a full rolling boil. Boil for 2 minutes. Add the sugar and stir well. Bring to a boil, stirring constantly, and boil for 4 minutes. Remove from the heat. Beat with rotary beater for 4 minutes. Cool, then pour into sterilized jars. Seal and refrigerate.

> ## Tip
> Strawberry jam made this way (just substitute strawberries for the raspberries) will blow you away!

Iced Bailey's Latte

Use frozen coffee cubes to dress up your glass of Bailey's Irish Cream. It's a match made in cocktail heaven with a simple twist!

3 COFFEE ICE CUBES (SEE TIP)

2 TABLESPOONS BAILEY'S IRISH CREAM LIQUEUR

¼ CUP PLAIN OR CHOCOLATE MILK

Pop the coffee ice cubes into a martini glass and top with Bailey's and milk. Gently stir and enjoy!

Tip

To make coffee ice cubes, brew fresh coffee. Cool completely before pouring into ice cube trays and freezing. Keep them on hand for this recipe or for any time you want iced coffee.

Jam & Cream Tarts

This versatile recipe is splendid with lemon curd, grape, raspberry, or blackberry jelly. Experiment to find your family's preferred flavor.

2 REFRIGERATED PIE CRUSTS (NOT IN A PIE PLATE)

14 OUNCES STRAWBERRY JAM

½ CUP HEAVY CREAM, WHIPPED

Preheat the oven to 350°F. Using a 2-inch round cookie cutter, cut out 24 rounds from the pie dough. Line 24 cups across 2 nonstick muffin tins. Drop approximately 1 tablespoon jam into each and bake until lightly golden, 12 to 15 minutes. Allow to cool, then transfer to a serving plate. When ready to serve, dollop each with a generous teaspoon of whipped cream.

Matchsticks

This is a childhood favorite. In times of trouble "Mother Mary" spoke to the Beatles. Matchsticks spoke to me!

Makes
8

2 SHEETS FROZEN PUFF PASTRY, THAWED

½ CUP STRAWBERRY JAM

1¼ CUPS HEAVY CREAM, WHIPPED

2 TABLESPOONS CONFECTIONERS' SUGAR

Preheat the oven to 400°F. Line a baking sheet with parchment paper. Place a sheet of pastry on the baking sheet. Top with another piece of parchment paper and another baking sheet (this keeps the pastry from rising too much). Bake until the pastry is crisp and golden, 15 to 20 minutes. Transfer to a wire rack to cool completely. Repeat with the second sheet of pastry. Use a sharp knife to cut 5 x 2-inch strips from the sheets. Spread the jam over half the pastry strips. Spread the whipped cream over the jam. Top with the remaining pastry. Dust with confectioners' sugar to serve.

Nutella Brownies

Nothing perks up my sweet tooth more than seeing the words "Nutella" and "brownies" next to each other.

1 CUP NUTELLA

1 LARGE EGG

5 TABLESPOONS ALL-PURPOSE FLOUR

¼ CUP HAZELNUTS, CHOPPED

Preheat the oven to 340°F. Line 12 cups of a mini-muffin pan with paper liners. In a medium bowl, stir together the Nutella and egg until combined and smooth. Mix in the flour. Spoon the batter into the muffin cups, filling them about three-fourths full. Sprinkle with the hazelnuts. Bake until a wooden skewer inserted into the center comes out with wet, gooey crumbs, about 12 minutes. Set on a rack to cool completely. Serve immediately or store in an airtight container at room temperature for up to 3 days.

Peanut Butter & Jelly Cookies

Makes
20

A classic combination and perfect for a child's party or even a proper afternoon tea.

1 CUP CRUNCHY PEANUT BUTTER

1 CUP RAW SUGAR

1 LARGE EGG

¼ CUP STRAWBERRY JELLY

Preheat the oven to 350°F. Line two baking sheets with parchment paper. In a medium bowl, mix together the peanut butter, sugar, and egg until nicely combined. Spoon tablespoon-size balls, 2-inches apart, onto the baking sheets. Using your thumb, make a well in each cookie. Fill each well with jam and bake until a thin crust forms on the cookies, about 8 minutes.

Optional

Swap the jelly for chocolate chips, a teaspoon of ground cinnamon, or, as my lovely editor, Sarah Branham's mom used to do, bake without anything inside the well. After you take the cookies out of the oven and let them cool for a few minutes, place a Hershey's Kiss in each well for some chocolate goodness. Love it!

 am so proud of this book and hope that it provides much inspiration for you in the years to come.

But, as with all things, it didn't just happen because of me. I have a brilliant team who works on these projects with me: researching, searching, sharing, cooking, crying, and laughing (mostly the latter, fortunately).

Thank you to my small but amazing team who make the 4 Ingredients series possible: Melinda, Michelle, and Kate, who keep the business running beautifully when I'm in lockdown mode, working on these projects. To Melanie, Nelly, and Leonie, you are such creative women; the pages within have been built from ideas you helped bring to life. To Skye at Sunny Girl Cakes for lending a hand and icing the pretty cupcakes that grace the front cover of this book. To Jennette, the most amazingly supportive Mum. Glen Turnbull, thank you for loving me every step of the way, and Sarah Branham, your attention to detail to ensure perfection in my books is truly appreciated.

I was going to send you all flowers but decided to make homemade treats instead: cupcakes, caramels, truffles, and cookies are on their way. I promise!

With love and gratitude,
Kim

COME SHARE A CUPPA WITH US

At 4 Ingredients, we have cultivated a global family of foodies bound together by the desire to create good, healthy, homemade meals quickly, easily, and economically. Our aim is to save us all precious time and money in the kitchen.

If this is you too, then we invite you to join our growing family where we share clever kitchen wisdom and delicious recipes daily. If you are looking for inspiration in the kitchen, then come say hello.

f **4ingredientspage**   @4ingredients   P @4ingredients   @4ingredients

You Tube **4 Ingredients Channel**   4 **4ingredients.com.au**

With love, Kim